JIMMY

STEWART

A Biography of the Iconic American Actor

Andrew Cooper

TABLE OF CONTENTS

JIMMY STEWART

Jimmy Stewart is a name known in Hollywood and throughout the world. He had a long, successful career and rose through the ranks in the movie industry to become one of the biggest names in acting. His style, his personality, and trademark stammering drawl and voice made him not only an ideal performer but also a trusted and beloved American citizen. He was and remains an actor that audiences truly cared for and believed in, a man who seemed decent and kind and honest. He wasn't the most glamorous or flashy performer of his time but there was always something genuine and homespun about Jimmy Stewart that transcended acting. He became more than just a movie legend; he became an *American* legend.

Stewart's impact on Hollywood is felt to this day, decades after the end of his career and his passing. He is heralded as one of the biggest legends to ever grace the big screen. Indeed, today it is the ultimate compliment to be called "the modern Jimmy Stewart." Why? Because that means you are a strong, hard-working performer with a steadfast set of values and a kind, gentle personality and determination to do your best in every role. Stewart's entire persona has come to define not only brilliant acting but also a summation of the ideal American.

He poured himself into his work and his time in Hollywood was filled with countless hits, but also many misses as well. His down-to-earth, humane performances, particularly his turn in the classic "It's A Wonderful Life," are still considered some of the best and most-beloved acting work the world has ever seen. In an era when so much of the acting was stilted or hammy, Stewart's work always felt authentic, gentle, and natural.

It wasn't just acting that Stewart was recognized for. His efforts during World War II were a testament to the decent, strong-willed man he was. He flew missions in the war and received several awards for his service. And when it was all over, he returned to the blossoming career he put on hold. He did this all when the option to stay safe behind the front lines was possible, when he could stay far from harm's way. Instead, he pleaded with his superiors to be put into battle and during the war, a war that would affect him greatly and haunt him for years to come.

Stewart remained Hollywood royalty until his death and his legacy remains all these years later. Though the industry has drastically changed and the sort of movies Stewart starred in aren't made anymore, he is still a gold standard when it comes to acting and attitude. There are few Hollywood legends as big as Jimmy Stewart.

But how did Stewart rise from his hometown in Pennsylvania to the highest ranks of Hollywood? How did he transform himself from a lackluster student who was destined to run his father's hardware store to a performer that the American Film Institute would call the third-greatest American actor of all time? It is a journey that is inspiring and truly uniquely American.

Early Life

James Maitland Stewart was born in Indiana, Pennsylvania on May 20, 1908. Indiana remains a small town and was even smaller at the time of Stewart's birth. With a population of just more than 5,000, Stewart didn't have much to do in his early years. The young Stewart spent most of his time going to church, studying for school and listening to his mother play piano.

Stewart was the only boy in his family. He had two younger sisters, born in 1912 and 1914 respectively. His father was Alexander Maitland Stewart and his mother was Elizabeth Ruth Stewart. Jimmy's father owned and operated J.M. Stewart and Company Hardware Store, the small business that had remained in the Stewart family for multiple generations. Jimmy's mother was a pianist and instilled a great love of music in the young boy, a passion he had for the rest of his life.

Jimmy's early home life was rather quiet and tame, led by his deeply religious father and caring, gentle mother. Jimmy was a shy boy, often lost in his daydreams instead of making friends or being social. Much of Jimmy's time was spent in his family basement, playing with his model airplanes and attempting to create mechanical drawings. At this age, Jimmy was invested in the idea of becoming a pilot. He wanted to enter the world of aviation instead of running the small hardware store that was being handed down to him.

Jimmy saw his desire to be a pilot as nothing more than a pipe dream. He knew what lay ahead for him. He would live a life much like his father and grandfather had. He wasn't that upset by the idea of spending his life in Indiana, Pennsylvania. In fact, he was quite content with his prospective future. It was the same tradition his father and his grandfather before him followed. Jimmy's world view was limited in scope but the young boy didn't seem to mind.

Indeed, his entire life and career seemed predetermined and set in stone. Jimmy's father was certain that his son would inherit the family business and spend the rest of his life in rural Pennsylvania. It was assumed he would find a wife, start a family and enjoy the rest of his days near his childhood home. After completing school, that is. While Jimmy's father wanted his son to take over the business and remain close to home, he was also intent on having his son attend Princeton before that. It was all laid out plainly for Jimmy and it seemed no decisions were his to make. If only Jimmy's parents knew the true path their son would take.

Convinced that Jimmy needed to attend a private school if he wished to enter Princeton, his parents enrolled the boy in Mercersburg Academy in Mercersburg, Pennsylvania in the fall of 1923. The academy is located about 90 miles northwest of Washington, D.C., and is a small, very respected college prep boarding school. Jimmy's parents knew how it would look to have their son be educated at such an institution and they pressed Jimmy to try his hardest and excel so that his future schooling career could be attained.

To everyone's surprise, the once-shy Jimmy began to come into his own while attending Mercersburg. He began to participate in extracurricular activities like joining the glee club, being art editor of the yearbook and running track. He also became heavily invested in playing football but, due to his small and skinny size, was only accepted to play on the third-tier team.

It wasn't always easy at Mercersburg and Stewart had a few setbacks. It was at this time that he officially gave up on his dreams of becoming a pilot as it became more and more apparent that his father would accept nothing less than a Princeton graduate.

Jimmy's health also took a hit during his time at prep school. In 1927, the young student was infected with scarlet fever but it quickly transformed into a kidney infection. It was a huge setback for Stewart, who was forced to take time out of school and delay his graduation until the spring of 1928. But even a medical issue as serious as that couldn't keep Stewart off track for long.

When Jimmy did return to Mercersburg, he would try his hand at something completely new: acting. In 1928, the young student appeared on stage in the play "The Wolves." It was Jimmy's first foray into performing. It definitely wouldn't be his last.

AN INTEREST IN ACTING

Jimmy Stewart finally made it to Princeton in 1928, where he began to study architecture and became a member of several clubs, including the Princeton Charter Club. It was at this time that Stewart also became involved with the Princeton Triangle Club. The Triangle Club is one of the premier theater troupes at Princeton. Founded in 1891 it remains one of the oldest college theater groups in the United States.

Joining the Triangle Club was a major move for Stewart and a sign that he was beginning to truly entertain the idea of acting after his college career concluded. He was torn, however, between pursuing a life in architecture, running his father's store back in Indiana, or attempting to make it as an actor. His life, which once had only one path, seemed to be expanding with possibility.

But in the end, Jimmy would graduate with his degree in architecture and an idea that he would follow the path laid out for him by his mother and father. Once again, he wasn't disappointed by this fate but there was a part of him yearning for something more, especially since he had found the power and joy he received from acting.

Jimmy Stewart graduated from Princeton at a troubled and challenging time for the country. The Great Depression was in full swing, leaving millions without jobs, food or homes. Jimmy didn't know what future awaited him now that the entire country was in disarray. So, he took the first offer he could find. A friend of his said that he could help prepare a Broadway play for the University Players, a summer stock theater company located in Cape Cop, Massachusetts. Jimmy took the position despite receiving a scholarship for graduate studies in architecture from Princeton. The fact that he was committing to the theater over his degree says a lot. Jimmy Stewart was being drawn deeper and deeper into the world of acting.

A Slow Start

The summer of 1932 would become the time that Jimmy Stewart fully and completely embraced his new found love of acting and began to pursue his desire to be a full-time actor. His work with the University Players was incredibly beneficial and monumental to him; it opened his eyes to how much he wanted a career in the performing field.

Working with the Players also gave Stewart a taste of young love. It was there that he met Margaret Sullavan, a young actress who instantly attracted Jimmy. While Stewart was instantly smitten with Sullavan, she regarded him only as a close friend. She was protective of the young actor and saw the talent inside him and wanted to help him further his career. Stewart, on the other hand, pined for Sullavan romantically. While Sullavan never entertained the idea of dating, she truly cared for young Jimmy and loved him.

Initially Stewart was mostly relegated to bit parts with the Players but his time working with them was still incredibly important to his young career. It was then that he worked with the company's directors, such as

Bretaigne Windust and Joshua Logan. Windust would go on to become an incredibly successful Broadway director while Logan would eventually win a Pulitzer Prize for co-writing "South Pacific." Jimmy Stewart was already making connections, connections that would help him shortly as his career began to bloom.

Jimmy also became friends with a young Henry Fonda who was also chasing his dream to become an actor. The two quickly struck up a close friendship that would last for decades.

When his first season with the University Players came to an end, Stewart decided to move to New York City with several acting friends, including Fonda. The life of an up-and-coming actor was tough but Stewart found work quickly and made his Broadway debut in the play "Carry Nation." The historical production, about temperance leader Carrie Nation, ended up being a major failure. It was a massive flop that only lasted for just 30 performances. However, it launched the career of several promising performers, including Stewart who portrayed Constable Gano alongside Myron McCormick, Joshua Logan, and Mildred Natwick.

From "Carry Nation," Stewart would go on to land another role. He was cast in "Goodbye Again" and his work in that play received notice from the media, including *The New Yorker*. It was the first taste of acclaim for Stewart and fully committed him to pursue his career further but it would require hard work and many false starts and possible failures.

His seven-month run in "Goodbye Again" came to an end but Stewart strove on to work more. After a brief stint in Boston, the hard-working young actor returned to New York and claimed several small roles, including a turn in "All Good Americans." But his career wasn't taking off as he had hoped, many of the productions he became involved with were not successful and ended up closing shortly after their debuts. He began thinking of giving up his dream, returning to school, or heading home to Pennsylvania to finally take over the family business.

"From 1932 through 1934, I'd only worked three months," Stewart would later say. "Every play I got into folded."

CAREER TAKE-OFF

I f it wasn't for the play "Yellow Jack," Jimmy Stewart would have never become the acting legend he was meant to be. It was that play that sent him on a path that would end with a permanent position in Hollywood history.

Stewart was about to throw in the towel and give up on his dreams of being an actor when he was cast in the docudrama "Yellow Jack," portraying Private John O'Hara, a soldier who undergoes experiments to cure Yellow Fever after the Spanish-American War. The production opened at the Martin Beck Theater in March 1934.

The play wasn't a runaway success but it was a modest hit and after a string of failures, that was a wonderful change for Jimmy. More importantly, Stewart's work in the play was praised by multiple critics. It was just what the doctor ordered. The play gave Stewart a boost in the desire to continue following his dreams and he threw out any ideas of heading back home, instead devoting himself full-time to becoming an actor.

The critical success from "Yellow Jack" opened a few more doors for Stewart and in the summer, he made his motion picture debut in a bit part in the film "Art Trouble." He continued doing theater and earned rave reviews for his turn in "Divided by Three." He also performed in the plays "We Die Exquisitely" and "All Paris Knows." He found success with the hit play "Page Miss Glory" but also found failure with the bomb "A Journey By Night" in Spring of 1935.

No matter if he appeared in a major hit or a major flop, Stewart was on a roll critically. He was continuously praised for his work on stage and this led to interest from Hollywood.

Talent scout Bill Grady had been following Stewart's career for a while by the end of 1935. An important and powerful figure in the movie industry, Grady was able to get Metro-Goldwyn-Mayer interested in the young actor and they signed him to a seven-year contract. This was a huge boon for Stewart, a kick start to his career that quite literally changed his life overnight. Leaving New York City for the bright lights of California, Stewart headed out west with a promising future ahead of him. Plans to take over his father's store or pursue a life as an architect quickly faded for good.

After landing in Los Angeles, Stewart shared an apartment with his pal Henry Fonda and began to act in films. His first Hollywood role would be in the Spencer Tracy film "The Murder Man" in 1935. His performance wasn't noticed by many and didn't jumpstart his career as he had hoped. MGM soon lost faith in the actor, seeing him as a supporting player rather than a traditional, handsome leading man. But Stewart's agent, Leland Hayward, had a plan. Hayward wanted Stewart loaned out to other studios who saw more potential in him. This move would later come back to greatly improve his career trajectory.

1936 would end up being a banner year for Stewart. Though MGM didn't know exactly what to do with him, the actor found success in his second film, "Rose Marie." From there, he found himself cast in seven other movies in just one year. Hollywood was taking notice of the young Jimmy Stewart but the road ahead would be supremely bumpy.

He was given a major assist from his fellow University Players alum and unrequited love Margaret Sullavan, who requested Stewart be cast opposite of her in "Next Time We Love." She still cared deeply for Jimmy and wanted to help him become a success. She also still believed in his talent and his ability to perform and now that she had some power in Hollywood, she used it. She fought to have Stewart cast alongside her in the motion picture and the move was a major moment for Jimmy.

The movie was a major hit and garnered the attention of the public, critics and MGM executives who had mostly written off the actor. He gained strong reviews from multiple major publications, most notably *The New York Times* and *Time Magazine*. This was Jimmy Stewart's first big break and it put him on a track to become a prominent star.

He would soon appear in multiple films in quick succession, including "Small Town Girl," "Important News," and "Wife vs. Secretary." He was making a name for himself but mostly with smaller, supporting roles. His first big leading part eluded him but Stewart didn't stop trying. His plucky and driven personality was coming in handy as he tried to make it as an actor.

Then came "Speed," a 1936 action film that gave Stewart his first starring role. The actor played auto mechanic and driver Terry Martin who was competing in the Indianapolis 500. Sadly, Stewart's first turn as a lead performer wasn't the hit he had hoped for. "Speed" ended up being both a critical and commercial flop. Reviews were lukewarm and little notice was given to Stewart. Still, the actor didn't lose faith or the drive to keep working. He still felt like his best and brightest days were ahead of him.

Unfortunately, the projects ahead were something of a mixed bag. While he did indeed land a leading role in "Born to Dance," critics were not kind to his work. The film required Stewart to sing and dance and his physical work was not met with much praise. His singing and dancing were actually called "painful."

However, Stewart was working so much at this time that the bad reviews didn't slow down his career, he simply plowed ahead into the next project and left the unfavorable mentions in the press behind him. Fortunately, his next film was "After the Thin Man." In it, Stewart played against type and portrayed a murderer. Unlike his work in "Born to Dance," his turn in this film was met with praise and had many critics thinking that perhaps there was more to Jimmy Stewart than what met the eye. This was his first instance of showing true depth and talent that wasn't suspected. Stewart loved trying something new and felt like he was finally showing his true potential for the first time in his budding career.

The next couple years would find Stewart appearing in many films such as "The Last Gangster," "Seventh Heaven," "Navy Blue and Gold" and more. But he was mostly appearing in smaller parts again. Despite a few false starts, it seemed possible that Jimmy Stewart would never become a full-on leading man in Hollywood.

The fact that MGM still had little faith in Stewart certainly didn't help. The studio was hesitant to cast Jimmy in any major parts and instead relegated him to minor parts that kept his career stalled. Stewart was growing frustrated by MGM's moves and their stranglehold on his future. However, Leland Hayward's plan to have Stewart lent out to other studios during this time finally paid off.

In 1938, Stewart was loaned by MGM to RKO to appear alongside his rumored girlfriend Ginger Rogers in "Vivacious Lady." The movie was going to be a big deal for Stewart and had the potential to finally skyrocket his career into the stratosphere. However, his success was immediately put into jeopardy because of health issues.

Stewart became seriously ill only days into shooting Vivacious Lady. The actor was hospitalized and production of the film was put on hold. RKO immediately shut down production due to Stewart's absence. When production was gearing up to begin again, RKO toyed with the idea of recasting Stewart's part but Rodgers refused to work alongside anyone else. RKO obliged and waited for Stewart to recover. He did and his performance in "The Vivacious Lady" was widely praised by critics and audiences. The film was also a major commercial hit too and made many more Americans take note of the young star. Stewart would forever feel indebted to Ginger Rogers for fighting for him and saving his career.

With the success of "Vivacious Lady" under his belt, Stewart was becoming a more recognizable name and while some of his next films weren't major hits, he was continually getting noticed by critics who praised his performances and called him one of the most talented young actors in Hollywood.

You Can't Take It with You

1938 would be Jimmy Stewart's year. When the actor was loaned out to Columbia Pictures, it set his career on a trajectory that would change his life forever. After years of hard work and multiple missed opportunities, things were finally lining up for him.

Stewart was cast in Frank Capra's film "You Can't Take It With You," starring opposite Jean Arthur. Stewart's inclusion in a Frank Capra film was a huge win for the actor. Capra was one of the biggest directors in Hollywood, having just released multiple enormous hits. He was a star-maker too, a director who could turn a supporting player into a leading man. The stamp of approval from Capra could not be understated, it had the chance to change lives. It just so happened that Capra was on the hunt for a new star when he came across Jimmy Stewart. He was instantly won over by the actor.

The film was a romantic comedy about a rich young man who falls in love with a poor and good-hearted woman. The movie was an absolute smash, a runaway success that finally launched Stewart's career like he had been hoping for. Just as he had hoped, working with Frank Capra has been a game changer for Jimmy Stewart.

"You Can't Take It With You" would end up becoming the fifth highest-grossing film of 1938 and was nominated for multiple Academy Awards. The movie would earn the coveted Best Picture Oscar. Between the commercial success, the critical praise and the awards, Jimmy Stewart finally found himself as one of the biggest names in Hollywood.

And his star would only get bigger, thanks again to Frank Capra.

"Mr. Smith Goes to Washington" was a political comedy-drama also directed by Capra that would enhance and strengthen Stewart's life and career even more. After working well with Stewart on "You Can't Take It With You," Capra cast the young rising star again. He was once again drawn to Stewart's charm, and personality, his everyman persona and salt-of-the-Earth charisma. He knew that Stewart would be perfect to play the lead role in the film.

"Mr. Smith Goes to Washington" revolves around an idealistic young politician who is thrown into the morally murky world of Washington. The film culminates in a long monologue about American ideals and doing the right thing and staying true to yourself. Capra knew Stewart would be excellent to deliver the role.

And he was. "Mr. Smith Goes to Washington" was a massive hit and ended up being the third highest-grossing film of 1939. Stewart's performance was praised from just about every critic and the movie made him an even bigger star. The film was nominated for multiple Academy Awards and Stewart himself was nominated for his first Best Actor

Oscar. Not only was Jimmy Stewart now a star, he was one of the biggest stars in the world.

Now that he was the top name in Hollywood, success was finding him again and again. "After Mr. Smith Goes to Washington," Stewart appeared in "Destry Rides Again" and "The Shop Around the Corner." He starred in several more movies, most of them hits, in 1939.

Off screen, Jimmy was dating and feeling the desire to settle down and find true love once and for all. He had seen multiple stars exclusively during his rise in Hollywood, including Ginger Rogers and Norma Shearer. Still, he was called the "Great American Bachelor" by gossip columnist and true intimacy and commitment eluded him.

Jimmy dated Loretta Young as his star was rising and implored her to settle down with him. However, Young was won over by other boyfriends and declined Jimmy's offer.

Stewart also had an affair with actress Marlene Dietrich, who was married when they met. Their relationship ended badly with rumors of a terminated pregnancy.

After those connections, Jimmy saw star Olivia de Havilland and even proposed marriage to her but she said no and feared that Jimmy wasn't really ready for the commitment. Like his stardom, his love life was full of false starts and shortcomings and it left him feeling dejected and alone.

But his career continued to find its footing. 1940 found Stewart starring in "The Philadelphia Story," a romantic comedy from director George Cukor. The film starred Jimmy Stewart and Katharine Hepburn, who was desperately looking for a hit after several of her previous films proved to be box office poison. "The Philadelphia Story" seemed poised to be a smash, a romantic comedy about a divorced couple who find love again. Stewart was cast as one of Hepburn's prospective romantic partners, Macaulay "Mike" Connor.

"The Philadelphia Story" was another giant success, a return to form for Hepburn and another victory for Stewart. The film raked in $2,374,000 in the United States, a massive sum at the time. The critics also raved about the movie, specifically calling out Stewart's charming comedic turn. "The Philadelphia Story" earned Stewart his second Oscar nomination.

Jimmy Stewart didn't think he would win the Academy Award and didn't plan to attend the ceremony. In fact, he voted for his close friend Henry Fonda in "The Grapes of Wrath." But then Stewart was advised to attend the awards and to wear a nice dinner jacket, suggesting he had a good chance at taking home the prize. Stewart felt like he was on the verge of a major turning point in his career.

Sure enough, on February 27, 1941 Jimmy Stewart won his first Oscar for "The Philadelphia Story." Despite the hint that he might win, Stewart was still shocked by the achievement. In later years, he would claim he thought his Oscar was a way to compensate for his loss for "Mr. Smith Goes to Washington." Regardless of *why* he won, his Oscar jettisoned his career even higher and made his star shine even brighter. Jimmy Stewart was arguably the biggest star in Hollywood as 1940 came to a close.

Despite all the fame and triumphs, Stewart hadn't forgotten where he came from and the people who helped him along the way. He gave his Oscar to his father, who displayed it to the public in the family store alongside other medals and awards. A piece of Indiana, Pennsylvania remained with Jimmy Stewart no matter how successful he became.

Jimmy kept working after his Academy Award win although his subsequent films did not prove to be the runaway hits that his previous ones were. Movies like "Come Live with Me" and "Pot o' Gold" did not bring in much box office cash. In fact, Stewart considered "Pot o' Gold" to be the worst movie in his filmography. Despite that, he continued on and didn't for one moment rest on his laurels or consider his goals met.

Stewart starred in the musical "Ziegfeld Girl" in 1941 as Gil the trucker driver. The movie, which told the story of three parallel women performing on Broadway, wasn't a critical hit but did find great success financially. If there was any doubt that Jimmy Stewart was the biggest actor working in Hollywood, it had been completely erased.

Stewart's next role wouldn't be on stage or screen, however. Up next for Jimmy Stewart was war.

WORLD WAR II

*"It may sound corny, but what's wrong with wanting to fight for your
country. Why are people reluctant to use the word patriotism?"*
- Jimmy Stewart

Jimmy Stewart enlisted in the military as America entered World War
II, much to the chagrin of MGM and other major studios. Stewart
was trying to honor a family tradition of serving and also wanted to
assist his country in their efforts to turn the tide of the war. He took it
seriously and was more committed to the fight abroad than to his life as
a performer.

Joining the military would also be Stewart's chance to finally become
the pilot he always dreamed of. In the years since college, Stewart had
become an amateur pilot and as he found success in Hollywood, he flew
more and more. It was nothing more than a fascinating hobby though,
nothing that he would make a career out of. But as the war loomed larger
over America, Stewart thought that flying could be his way to help
America.

Stewart officially enlisted in March 1941 and was assigned to the Air Corps. Originally, Stewart was drafted into the Army but was then rejected because he was underweight. It seemed his famous lanky and thin build was working against him. But his 400 training hours of flying in civilian life assisted him with the Air Corps and he began to take basic flight training and earned his pilot wings shortly thereafter. Stewart earned his position as second lieutenant in early 1942.

Stewart's acting career was put on hold after his enlistment. In fact, it would be years before he would return to Hollywood and act again. During his time with the military, Stewart made public appearances on behalf of the Army Air Force. He dropped in at radio stations to give interviews and boost morale and enlistment. He also appeared in a short film titled "Winning Your Wings" in 1942. The film, which would later be nominated for Best Documentary at the Academy Awards, would bring in 150,000 new recruits. Even in the military, Stewart's presence in front of the camera had an effect on audiences.

Stewart spent the next year training young pilots before sending them off to war. It was a rewarding job and one that was majorly important to the effort but Stewart grew concerned that he was going to be relegated to jobs that were far from the front lines. Jimmy Stewart wanted to get in the fight, he wanted to help his country. He wasn't there to observe from the side.

Stewart appealed to his superiors, pleading with them to allow him to fly in the war and leave the training behind. They agreed and Stewart was sent to England with the 445th Bombardment Group in November 1943. He was tasked with piloting a B-24 Liberator, which was a heavy bomber plane. The B-24 was a mammoth plane, a vehicle that could hold a small crew and several massive bombs inside. It was a plane that would definitely see serious action overseas and Stewart's assignment with one guaranteed that his days of being off the front lines were over.

On January 7, 1944, Stewart was part of a bombing mission in Ludwigshafen, Germany. Something went wrong over the skies of Germany but Stewart's calm and steady demeanor saved lives and earned him praise. In the midst of battle, Stewart chose to not break formation from other bombing planes that had gotten off track from their planned route. Stewart could have stayed on the right course and abandoned the other planes but instead he and his group of bombers stayed with them during heavy fire. Considerable damage was inflicted on 48 of Stewart's aircrafts but he saved many from annihilation by choosing to stay and protect his fellow airmen.

Stewart's bravery and smart thinking earned him the Distinguished Flying Cross from the U.S. Armed Forces. The medal is one of the highest in all the military and is given to those who show acts of heroism while participating in aerial flight. He also received the Croix de guerre from the French military and the Air Medal for his act of heroism.

There were other dangerous missions that didn't go as well as the events over Ludwigshafen. Multiple other missions in Germany caused the deaths of many of Stewart's men. Stewart saw dozens of his peers lost in battle, shot down on missions they flew into alongside him. And because of his rising rank, Stewart was tasked with writing to the parents of those who perished. The actor was seeing firsthand the cruel and brutal world of war. The glitz and glamor of Los Angeles couldn't have seemed further away during those dark days of World War II.

The high-risk, dangerous world of war was understandably draining on the actor and had an effect on his mental well-being in the midst of combat. Reports from soldiers who flew with Stewart said that on several occasions, the actor showed signs of being shell shocked or battle fatigued. He was exhibiting symptoms of what we now call Post Traumatic Stress Disorder (PTSD) and the stress of war was getting to him. His fellow men said he wasn't afraid of dying or the bombs and bullets. Instead, Stewart had a severe fear of making a mistake and causing the death of one of his peers. Like it did for so many soldiers, the war was taking its toll on Jimmy Stewart.

Despite the harsh conditions and treacherous emotional damage being inflicted on him, Stewart was a wonderful pilot and proved that he wasn't just a talented actor spending time away from Hollywood. He was promoted to full colonel in March 1945. His rise through the ranks made him one of a few select American service members who went from private to colonel in only four years. Stewart had finally flown like he had always dreamed, made his family proud and helped his country win the war.

As the war wound down and Stewart imagined a life after the military, Hollywood was on the forefront of his mind. But it had been multiple years since he had acted on the big screen, would he be accepted back? Additionally, as World War II ended it became obvious to Stewart and others around him that perhaps the war had changed the Oscar winner.

Although Stewart would remain involved with the military for the rest of his life, his time in World War II came to an end in early fall 1945, when the actor returned home to the United States. What came next was up in the air.

RETURN FROM
WAR AND HOLLYWOOD

Jimmy Stewart was experiencing serious doubts about his career as he returned to the United States after the war. He was still a hot commodity in Hollywood and was wanted by legions of studios and directors. Yet the Oscar winner wasn't sure if he wanted to act anymore. He toyed with the idea of giving up his profession and finally heading home to Pennsylvania to take control of his family store. A great debate raged inside him.

It is hard to tell what exactly caused Stewart's reluctance to consider acting. Many speculate that his time in World War II had a serious impact on him and sent him into a post-war depression. Indeed, those close to him say he wasn't quite himself after his tours overseas.

Others think it was the retirement of his agent Leland Hayward that caused Stewart to contemplate giving up acting. Despite his doubts about his future, Stewart signed a contract with Music Corporation of America.

But his drive to perform was diminished and he was continually thinking of giving it all up and returning home to Pennsylvania.

But then fate intervened and put Jimmy back on track. Stewart's collaborator Frank Capra came to him with a project titled "It's a Wonderful Life." Capra, who was also returning to Hollywood after spending the last few years making war documentaries, thought that Stewart was flawless for the lead role of George Bailey. In the film, Bailey is a small-town family man who has grown frustrated and angry at his boring, ordinary lot in life. He is a sour, bitter man who takes it out on his family and loved ones. He plans to commit suicide on Christmas Eve but is then shown an alternative world where he never existed, a world that desperately needs George Baily. The film concludes by being an inspirational tale about the importance of family, friends, faith and belief in yourself.

The role of Bailey played to Stewart's strengths as a likable, relatable common man. Unknown to others, the role also capitalized on many of the doubts and angers that Stewart was feeling after the war. Even though he signed on to star in the movie for Capra, the actor was still considering retirement and was doubting himself and growing frustrated with his work and career.

Filming of "It's a Wonderful Life" began on April 15, 1946. It was Stewart's first post-war role and his return to acting was met with challenges he didn't expect. He felt rusty and unsure of himself throughout production but the faith that Capra and the rest of the crew had in him kept him going. Production wrapped a few months later and the film entered general release on December 20, 1946.

The film was one of a few that touched upon dramatic and heartfelt themes following the war. The reviews were not that strong, remaining mixed at best. Some of the reviews, like the one from *Time Magazine*, were quite glowing while others were mostly dismissive. Capra's plot was criticized by many as being too saccharine and sentimental. However, despite some negative remarks about the film as a whole, Stewart's performance was usually praised. Hollywood and the country had missed Jimmy Stewart and welcomed him back with glee.

The film received a mixed reception and wasn't originally a hit with audiences either. In fact, it barely broke even upon its release despite the love of Stewart. Regardless, the movie was nominated for five Academy Awards that year, including Best Picture and another nomination for Stewart as Best Actor.

Although he had his doubts about the work he did in "It's a Wonderful Life," the role would go on to define him in many ways. His warm persona shone through in every scene, even in those when he is angry and cruel. In years since the film's release, the scenes that show a joyful and loving George Bailey have come to perfectly summarize the attributes for which Stewart is best remembered. In later years, Stewart would claim it was his favorite work in his filmography. The movie has grown into a true Christmas masterpiece and something that is regularly shown on television annually. It is hard to think of a holiday classic that is more enjoyed and cherished than "It's a Wonderful Life."

The movie was noticed by many even though the initial reception was muted. Even President Truman remarked on Stewart's performance. Despite all this praise, the Oscar nomination, and his eventual love for the movie, Stewart still had his doubts about his own acting after "It's a Wonderful Life." These feelings were magnified by the changing landscape of Hollywood. The era that Stewart had entered with was fading and being replaced by young actors such as James Dean, Marlon Brando and more. These actors were not like Stewart, they approached their craft in a completely different way and were known for roles that were grittier, darker and more challenging to audiences. Stewart, who had crafted himself into America's favorite nice guy, did not see where he fit in the industry. His doubts increased and, once again, America's favorite everyman questioned his next steps.

Perhaps because of this inner conflict, Stewart returned to the stage in 1947. He appeared in the play "Harvey" by Mary Coyle Chase and received universal praise. The actor felt a comfort and ease performing in front of crowds that he rarely found when making a movie. It reminded him of what he loved about acting and centered his inner turmoil.

It was during this time that Stewart first met Gloria Hatrick McLean at a Christmas party. At first, Stewart did not leave a good impression on Gloria because he drank far too much at the party and became quite drunk. But Stewart was struck by McLean's beauty and personality and, after meeting again thanks to actor Gary Cooper and his wife Veronica, the two began to date. The inclusion of Gloria in his life gave Jimmy the sort of love, affection and care that he had longed for. Even when his acting world was troubled and confusing, Gloria gave him great clarity.

A CHANGE IN DIRECTION

"Learn from the masters, learn from your contemporaries.
Always try to update yourself." - Jimmy Stewart

Jimmy Stewart was seeking a career revival and renewal as the 1940s came to a close. He was tired of playing the same old parts and felt that he was being typecast. He wanted to expand his horizons and try some new things. He needed to inject a new energy into his storied career.

Luckily, that was when he met Alfred Hitchcock.

Hitchcock cast Stewart in his 1948 psychological thriller "Rope." The movie, which was filmed in a series of long takes without interruption, was a challenge for Stewart in many ways. The filming technique made the movie feel more like a play than a motion picture. Also, Stewart's part was very different from his previous roles. Stewart played a retired teacher who engages with a pair of young killers.

Stewart's part was darker than the type of character he usually played and audiences saw him in a new light. This was the sort of direction Stewart had wanted since he noticed the rise of Marlon Brando and other younger performers.

Unfortunately, "Rope" garnered mixed reviews upon release and some said that Stewart was miscast and didn't fit the part, not for lack of trying. The pressure from filming and the picture's reception led Stewart to feel stressed out and exasperated. He also drank more after the film's release. Clearly, he wasn't feeling comfortable in Hollywood despite all his success.

Though "Rope" didn't end up like he had hoped, Stewart admired Hitchcock and enjoyed working with him and was honored by the faith the director put in him. This budding relationship would prove very fruitful in the years to come.

Stewart's career was headed in a different direction right as his personal life was as well. Jimmy and Gloria had continued to date for a couple of years and were married on August 9, 149 at the Brentwood Presbyterian Church in Los Angeles. The couple bought a luxury home in Beverly Hills and Stewart adopted Hatrick's two children from a previous marriage, Ronald and Michael and then had twin daughters in 1951.

SUCCESS IN THE 1950S

As the 1950s began, Stewart was still insistent on charting a new path for himself. He jumped on the Western bandwagon that was taking Hollywood by storm and appeared in multiple films in that genre, including "Winchester '73" and "Broken Arrow." These movies saw Stewart as the type of characters he had never approached before. Both films, especially "Winchester '73," proved to be major hits at the box office. It seemed audiences were comfortable seeing Stewart in a different light.

He followed those hits with "The Jackpost" and then, in December 1950, a film adaptation of "Harvey." Having starred in the Broadway play, Stewart felt prepared to take on the feature film version of the story. However, Stewart would later say he was dissatisfied with his turn in "Harvey" and felt he could have done things quite differently. He was also disappointed in the movie's initial reception, which was lukewarm at best. However, the movie would gain popularity in following years and despite mixed marks from audiences and critics, Stewart earned another Academy Award nomination for his work on "Harvey."

Stewart continued to work with director Anthony Mann in the subsequent years. In fact, he made four more Westerns with the filmmaker in the early 1950s, including "The Naked Spur" and "Bend of the River." These movies were all quite successful with the general public and showed a more developed and edgier side of Stewart. He was finally able to achieve the sort of depth and range he had been hoping to show for years. The success of these films led to a career revival for Stewart and gave the actor a serious boost in morale. Mann and Stewart worked together on a few non-Western projects as well, including the critically acclaimed "The Glenn Miller Story." That movie told the tale of famed band leader Glenn Miller and his career and subsequent service in World War II. Stewart received much praise for his take on Miller and also earned a BAFTA nomination for his performance.

Stewart began to work more extensively with Alfred Hitchcock and created a couple of wildly successful movies in the mid-to-late 1950s. It started with 1954's "Rear Window," a thriller about a photographer who becomes paranoid and suspicious of his neighbors while stuck at home with a broken leg. The film was a bona fide smash and went on to be the third biggest movie of the year.

Working with Hitchcock was a rewarding experience once again and Stewart found himself exploring new depths and reaching new heights with his acting abilities. His work was met with critical acclaim and his relationship with Hitchcock continued to be fruitful. 1956 saw them release "The Man Who Knew Too Much," another hit. Their working relationship culminated with "Vertigo," a 1958 thriller that is now considered one of the greatest works from both artists. Stewart's performance in "Vertigo" was a hit with critics but the movie itself did not perform as well as "Rear Window" and "The Man Who Knew Too Much."

Hitchcock seemingly soured on Stewart at this time and felt he was becoming too old to take on certain roles. Stewart attempted to be cast in Hitchcock's "North by Northwest" but Hitchcock instead chose to cast Cary Grant, who was a few years younger than Stewart.

While the end of his collaborative relationship with Alfred Hitchcock was disappointing, Stewart now had a newfound faith in himself and continued to work hard throughout the 1950s. He took on movies like "The Man from Laramie," once again with director Anthony Mann, "Night Passage," and "Bell, Book and Candle."

The decade would end with Stewart starring in "Anatomy of a Murder," an intense courtroom drama that saw Stewart portray a small-town lawyer drawn into a gritty and brutal murder case. Reviews for Stewart's work in "Anatomy of a Murder" were wonderful across the board and the movie earned him his fifth and final Academy Award nomination as well as his first BAFTA.

The 1950s concluded with Stewart as one of the biggest draws in all of Hollywood. Though it started with struggle and personal conflict, the decade was his most successful and has put Stewart back on a top in a very major way.

LATER YEARS

Jimmy Stewart entered the 1960s — and his 50s — with wind in his sails and a newfound faith from both himself and audiences who had seen the actor take on varied roles over the last decade.

Though he had appeared in dramas, thrillers and romantic comedies throughout his career, it would be the Western genre that would prove most fruitful as the 60s began. With his close relationship with Alfred Hitchcock over, Stewart began to work closely with director John Ford. Their first collaboration was "Two Rode Together" in 1961. He would then go on to work with Ford on "How the West Was Won," a Western epic that generated huge numbers at the box office. Stewart stayed within the Western genre when he co-starred alongside John Wayne in John Ford's "The Man Who Shot Liberty Valance." The movie is now considered one of the best Westerns ever made and was a major event upon its release because of its top billing of Wayne and Stewart, together on screen for the first time.

The 60s was a busy and mostly successful time for the Oscar winner. He appeared in other movies as the decade wore on, movies like "The Mountain Road," "Take Her," "She's Mine," and "Mr. Hobbs Takes a Vacation." He also co-starred in John Ford's final Wester film, "Cheyenne Autumn," in which he portrayed Wyatt Earp.

He would work in other pictures throughout the decade but it was Westerns that took up most of his time. He appeared in "Firecreek" with his dear friend Henry Fonda, "Bandolero!," "The Rare Breed" and "The Cheyenne Social Club." The busy decade was wearing him out and Stewart slowed down his screen appearances as the 1970s approached.

THE JIMMY STEWART
SHOW AND RETIREMENT

Jimmy Stewart's age was catching up with him as the 70s began. The last couple decades had seen Stewart become the biggest star in the world as well as a husband, father and soldier. His non-stop work schedule was having its impact on the actor and he was looking for a change of pace.

"The Jimmy Stewart Show" was an NBC sitcom that was most definitely a wild difference from what Stewart was used to. Stewart thought it would provide the sort of tempo he and his family needed as the actor approached his mid-60s.

The series saw Stewart starring as anthropology professor James K. Howard who invites his son and family to come live with him after their house burns down. NBC was elated to sign Stewart to a regular series but the sitcom itself didn't provide anything new to the medium and received poor reviews and even poorer ratings.

For his part, Stewart ended up being quite unhappy working on the sitcom and felt that it demanded more work than he expected. Luckily for him, the series was canceled after just one season.

Stewart starred in "Fools' Parade" in 1971, another Western that earned Stewart some of the best reviews of his later career.

Stewart's work after "Fools' Parade" consisted of a television version of "Harvey" in 1972 and the CBS mystery series "Hawkins" in 1973. "Hawkins" found Stewart portraying a small-town lawyer digging into murder cases. His work on the show, which only lasted one season, won him a Golden Globe.

Stewart continued to slow in the mid-70s. He performed on stage again in a London production of Harvey and had a supporting part in John Wayne's final movie, "The Shootist." His other work consisted of supporting roles, like those in "Airport '77" and "The Big Sleep."

Stewart turned down multiple roles at this time, like starring ones in "On Golden Pond" and "Network." He instead chose to spend time with his family and appear occasionally on television talk shows, most notably "The Tonight Show with Johnny Carson." It was on that show that Stewart showed a new hobby: poetry.

Stewart had begun writing poetry earlier in his life but was only truly comfortable sharing his work on Carson's show in the 80s. He recited one of his poems, an ode to his late family dog, on July 28, 1981. His performance of that poem touched Carson, who was visibly moved by it. Stewart's collected poems would eventually be collected in the book *Jimmy Stewart and His Poems*, which was released in 1989.

FINAL YEARS ON SCREEN

The 1980s were a relatively quiet time for Jimmy Stewart's career. The actor stated that he had semi-retired and spent most of his time with family and friends rather than on screen.

His few appearances throughout that decade featured work in a couple of TV movies: HBO's "Right of Way" and the holiday film "Mr. Krueger's Christmas." He also used his talent for some commercial work, providing voice over performances for Campbell's Soup commercials. But most of his appearances consisted of his time with Johnny Carson or on other talk shows. It seemed that Jimmy Stewart really was wrapping up his career.

Jimmy Stewart's final film performance would be in the animated movie "An American Tail: Fievel Goes West." He starred as a dog named Sheriff Wylie Burp and delivered all of his lines with the classic Stewart drawl and voice that people had come to love over the last forty years.

Though Stewart stopped acting, he was still present at multiple awards shows throughout the 80s as the industry saluted him for his classic work and impact on Hollywood. He received Kennedy Center

Honors in 1982, an Academy Honorary Award in 1985, an American Film Institute Award in 1980 as well as recognition from the National Board of Review and Film Society of Lincoln Center.

One of Stewart's greatest honors was receiving the Presidential Medal of Freedom from Ronald Reagan in 1985. The award, which is given for "contributions in the fields of arts, entertainment and public service" is the highest civilian award in the United States.

LATER YEARS AND DEATH

Jimmy Stewart had officially retired from acting as the 80s came to a close. He spent all of his time with his family and his wife Gloria, who began to experience serious medical problems in her older age.

Gloria was diagnosed with lung cancer in the early 90s and her health declined rapidly. After nearly 50 years together, Jimmy said goodbye to Gloria on February 16, 1994 when she lost her battle to cancer.

Understandably, the loss of his great love had a massive impact on the aged star and many said that he grew depressed, quiet and "lost at sea." His family remarked that Stewart withdrew from not only public life, but private life too. He did not interact much with friends and much family after the passing of Gloria and spent his time alone in his bed room.

Stewart's own health began to fail shortly after Gloria's. In 1995, Jimmy suffered a fall and was hospitalized briefly. He had received a pacemaker years before which was due to have its battery changed in late 1996 but the actor, ready for his storied life to come to an end, refused the procedure and in 1997 he was hospitalized for an irregular heartbeat.

Jimmy was hospitalized again on June 25, 1997 due to a pulmonary embolism as a result of a thrombosis in his right leg. One week later, on July 2, 1997 Jimmy Stewart passed away surrounded by his children at his home in Beverly Hills, California. The screen legend was 89 years old.

Jimmy's final words were allegedly "I'm going to be with Gloria now."

Tributes and personal stories about Stewart came pouring in after his death. Newspapers around the country celebrated the star and posted his picture on front pages. Even President Bill Clinton released an official state on the actor's passing. Hailed as a national treasure by countless people, Stewart's life and career were celebrated in multiple television specials and remembrances. After years of hard work and countless successes on the big screen and stage, Stewart's place in Hollywood history was assured.

Jimmy Stewart was buried at Forest Lawn Memorial Park in Glendale, California. More than 3,000 mourners attended a memorial service for the Oscar winner, including stars such as Bob Hope and Carol Burnett.

Johnny Carson's statement about his friend Jimmy summed the actor up perfectly: "He was one of the nicest, most unassuming persons I have known in my life."

LEGACY

To this day, Jimmy Stewart is often heralded as the ultimate Hollywood nice guy. The word "everyman" is used to describe the star regularly as well. Perhaps the strongest part of his legacy is that: that there is something that seemed so normal and relatable about Stewart.

From his voice and look to the roles he took to his off-screen personality Stewart did not seem like a typical actor. He did not seem larger than life and unbelievably good-looking. Instead, there were many things people saw in Stewart that they also saw in their friends and neighbors.

Those attributes were a big deal when Stewart first came on the scene. The country was not used to actors and actresses who felt cut from the same cloth as them. They always expected performers from the big screen to seem almost god-like and impossibly handsome and beautiful. Stewart was one of the first stars to truly seem like an average person. This was highlighted by many of the roles he took. From "It's A Wonderful Life" to "The Man Who Shot Liberty Valance" and many more, Stewart was playing people who felt grounded in reality.

But there was so much more to Stewart than his personality and disarming stuttering style of speech and the relatable roles he chose. Stewart's career was also filled with performances that were challenging and daring, like some of his work with John Ford or Alfred Hitchcock or his turn in "Anatomy of a Murder."

Because of the trust and affinity Stewart built with audiences throughout the years, his later, edgier work was seen as more believable and lived in. Stewart was able to carry that compassionate and lovable demeanor into work that was darker and tougher. He was able to explore his true acting skills and audiences were happy to come along with him.

One of the biggest parts of Jimmy Stewart's legacy is that he was never truly satisfied with his work and consistently pushed himself to do better and do more. Even when he was the most successful actor in Hollywood, he still yearned to try something hard and new. He never wanted to be typecast or seem like a one-trick-pony. He understood his strong suits in acting and he worked hard to improve his weak points too. He was an actor who took his craft seriously and remained kind, loving and gentle through it all. His ego never seemed inflated and he never grew out of touch. And his career was constantly striving to grow.

To this day, Jimmy Stewart is considered one of the greatest American actors to ever live. And while many will point to his charming style and voice and personality, his iconic legacy has stood the test of time because of much more than that. Jimmy Stewart was an actor's actor, someone who rose through the ranks of theater to the big screen.

Jimmy Stewart worked hard at all he did, a testament to the man who truly wanted to be his best at all times. He had quite a few setbacks and failures and wasn't always a sure thing. Critics, audiences and even studios wrote him off as a supporting actor at best. Even Stewart himself had his doubts. But he did not let that stop him. Instead, he invested time and energy in working harder and building successful creative relationships to raise himself to another level. He did all of this while maintaining a decent home life and raising a family and remaining devoted to his loving wife, Gloria. He also achieved great stardom while fighting for his country even though he could have chosen to stay off the front lines and watch the war from afar.

There are many reasons to respect Jimmy Stewart. He can be admired for the man he was off screen to the performer he was on screen. His impact is still felt to this day. He leaves behind a filmography filled with vast variety and multiple classic performances. And he leaves behind a legacy of a man who cared about his family and his craft and never compromised either.

Printed in Great Britain
by Amazon

53077273R00030